I0845213

Allure

Allure

Meditations on social constructs while tying flies.

Volume I: Works 1–15

William Jude Rumley

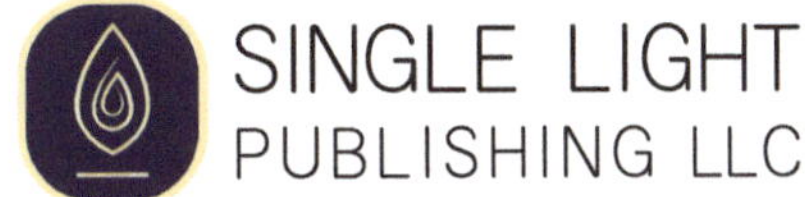

SINGLE LIGHT
PUBLISHING LLC

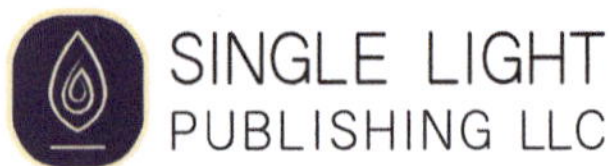

SINGLE LIGHT
PUBLISHING LLC

For my beloved Rebecca

Your love, your steadfast support, and the artistry you shared in editing and design brought this project to life.

List of Works

Allure Series

Allure: verb, powerfully attract or charm; tempt.

At this point in my life I identify as a self-proclaimed extraordinarily adequate fly fisher and flytier. I have spent many years learning to tie my own flies—learning through mimicry of many well-known, published fly fishers.

I have come to think of the practice of fly fishing as a form of puppetry. The puppeteer creates the puppet, as object, and then simulates life by imparting life through mimicry in movement, as performance, to engage the audience and convey a message or narrative.

In fly fishing the audience is not man but beast.

The practice of fly tying is a very repetitive and meditative process.

During these meditative times, I came to the realization that I could combine my art practice with fly tying. My work as an artist has been based in storytelling and theatrical devices. My work of the past and present is performance in nature, presented most often through mechanical reproductions of form through the use of indexical media.

My objective, in regard to my work as an artist, is to explore my understanding of art making and to critique social constructs often not apparent due to our systemic blindness.

–William Jude Rumley

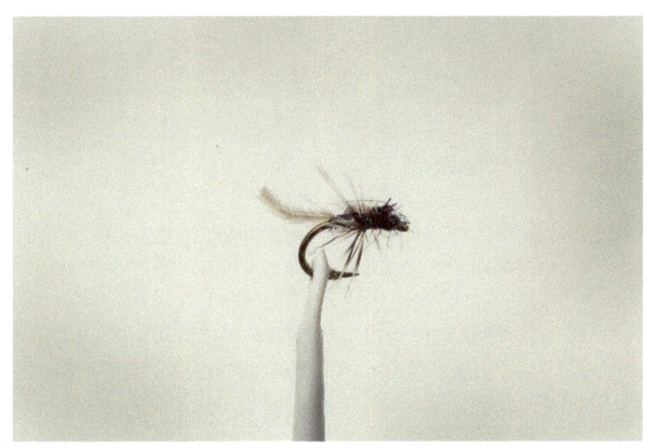

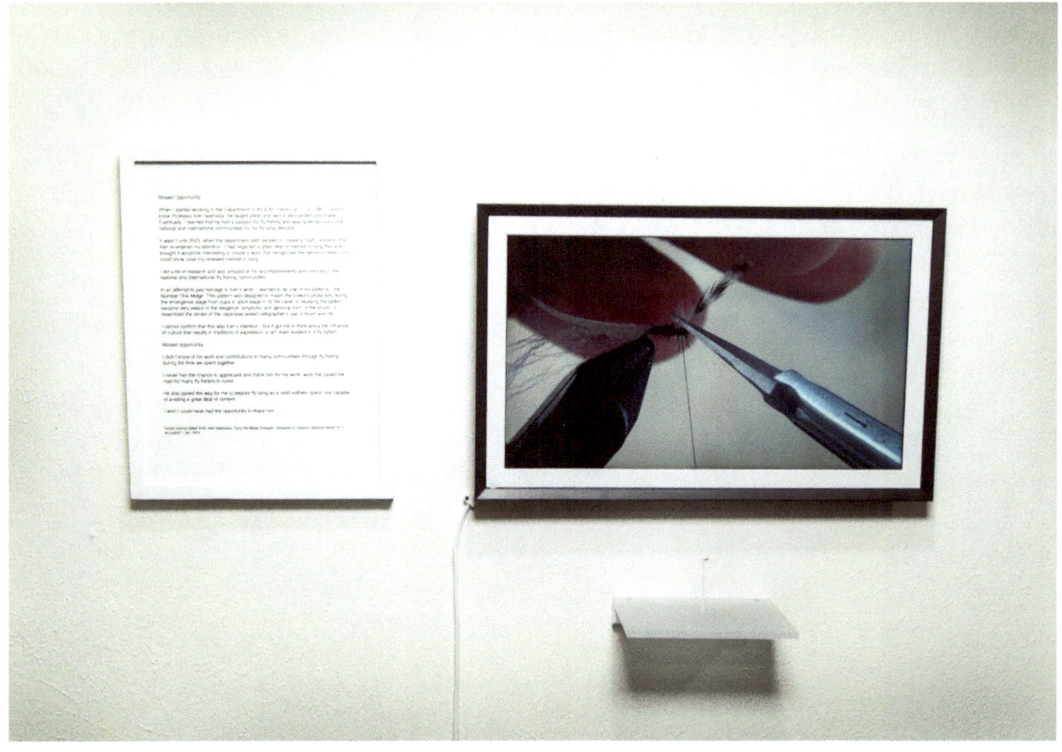

01. Missed Opportunity

When I started working in the Department of Art & Art History at CU in 1989, I came to know Professor Ken Iwamasa. He taught photo and was a very skilled print maker. Eventually, I learned that he had a passion for fly fishing and was quite famous in the national and international communities for his fly tying designs.

It wasn't until 2023, when the department staff decided to create a Staff Exhibition, that Ken re-entered my attention. I had regained a great deal of interest in tying flies and I thought it would be interesting to create a work that recognized the retired professor and could show case my renewed interest in tying.

I did a bit of research and was amazed at his accomplishments and notoriety in the national and international fly fishing communities.

In an attempt to pay homage to Ken's work, I learned to tie one of his patterns—the Number One Midge. This pattern was designed to match the insect's physicality during the emergence stage from pupa to adult stage in its life cycle. In studying the pattern, I became very aware of the elegance, simplicity, and gestural form of the shuck—it resembled the stroke of the Japanese skilled calligrapher's use of brush and ink.

I cannot confirm that this was Ken's intention. But it got me to think about the influence of culture that results in traditions of expression in art, even evident in a fly pattern.

Missed opportunity.

I didn't know of his work and contributions to many communities through fly fishing during the time we spent together.

I never had the chance to appreciate and thank him for his work; work that paved the road for many fly fishers to come.

He also paved the way for me to explore fly tying as a valid esthetic quest, one capable of availing a great deal of content.

I wish I could have had the opportunity to thank him.

Link to video

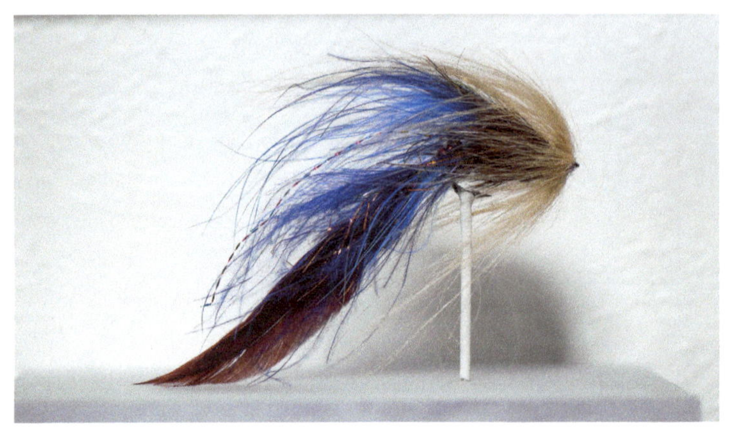

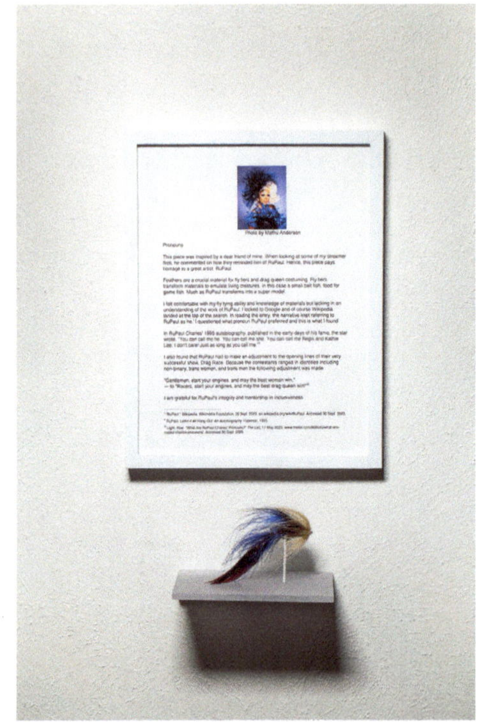

Photo by Mathu Andersen

Pronouns

This piece was inspired by a dear friend of mine. When looking at some of my streamer flies, he commented on how they reminded him of RuPaul. Hence, this piece pays homage to a great artist, RuPaul.

Feathers are a crucial material for fly tiers and drag queen costuming. Fly tiers transform materials to emulate living creatures, in this case a small bait fish, food for game fish. Much as RuPaul transforms into a super model.

I felt comfortable with my fly tying ability and knowledge of materials but lacking in an understanding of the work of RuPaul. I looked to Google and of course Wikipedia landed at the top of the search. In reading the entry, the narrative kept referring to RuPaul as he.[1] I questioned what pronoun RuPaul preferred and this is what I found.

In RuPaul Charles' 1995 autobiography, published in the early days of his fame, the star wrote, "You can call me he. You can call me she. You can call me Regis and Kathie Lee. I don't care! Just as long as you call me."[2]

I also found that RuPaul had to make an adjustment to the opening lines of their very successful show, Drag Race. Because the contestants ranged in identities including non-binary, trans women, and trans men the following adjustment was made.

"Gentlemen, start your engines, and may the best woman win."
— to "Racers, start your engines, and may the best drag queen win!"[3]

I am grateful for RuPaul's integrity and mentorship in inclusiveness.

[1] "RuPaul." Wikipedia, Wikimedia Foundation, 26 Sept. 2025, en.wikipedia.org/wiki/RuPaul. Accessed 30 Sept. 2025.
[2] RuPaul. Lettin it all hang out: an autobiography. Hyperion, 1995.
[3] Light, Alan. "What Are RuPaul Charles' Pronouns?" The List, 17 May 2023, www.thelist.com/808540/what-are-rupaul-charles-pronouns/. Accessed 30 Sept. 2025.

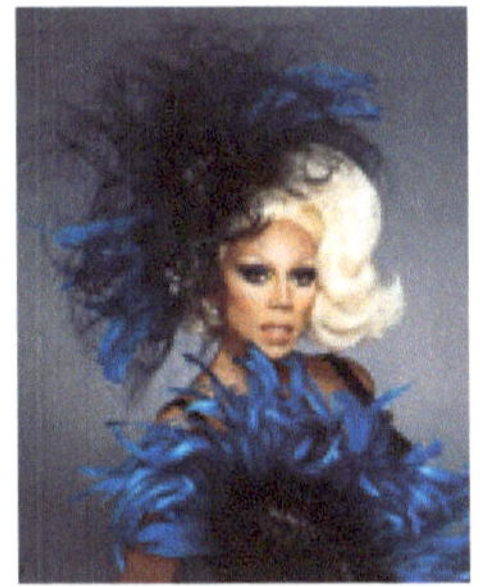

Photo by Mathu Anderson

02. Pronouns

This piece was inspired by a dear friend of mine. When looking at some of my streamer flies, he commented on how they reminded him of RuPaul. Hence, this piece pays homage to a great artist, RuPaul.

Feathers are a crucial material for fly tiers and drag queen costuming. Fly tiers transform materials to emulate living creatures, in this case a small bait fish, food for game fish. Much as RuPaul transforms into a super model.

I felt comfortable with my fly tying ability and knowledge of materials but lacking in an understanding of the work of RuPaul. I looked to Google and of course Wikipedia landed at the top of the search. In reading the entry, the narrative kept referring to RuPaul as he. I questioned what pronoun RuPaul preferred and this is what I found:

In RuPaul Charles' 1995 autobiography, published in the early days of his fame, the star wrote, "You can call me he. You can call me she. You can call me Regis and Kathie Lee; I don't care! Just as long as you call me."

I also found that RuPaul had to make an adjustment to the opening lines of their very successful show, Drag Race. Because the contestants ranged in identities including non-binary, trans women, and trans men the following adjustment was made:

"Gentlemen, start your engines, and may the best woman win."
— to "Racers, start your engines, and may the best drag queen win!"

I am grateful for RuPaul's integrity and mentorship in inclusiveness.

Reference:
RuPaul. *Lettin' it All Hang Out: An Autobiography.* Hyperion, 1995.

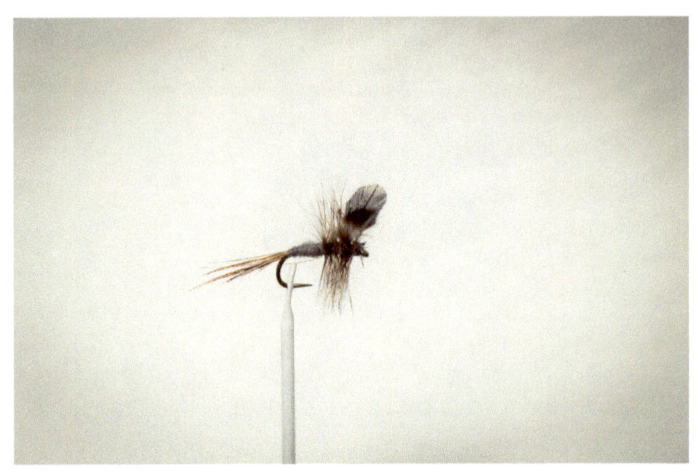

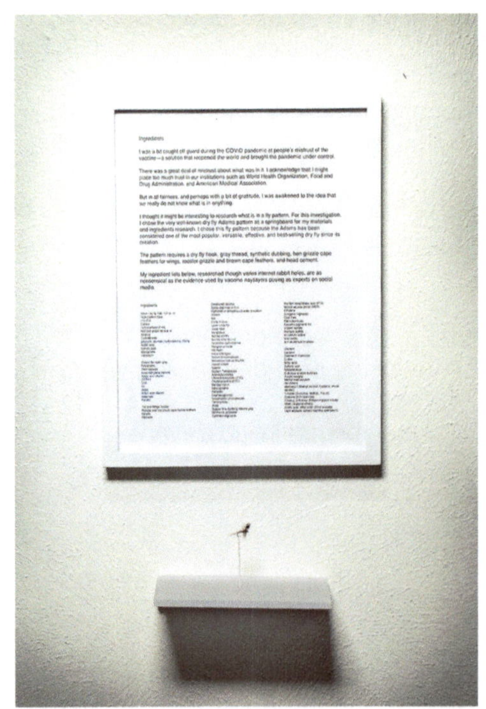

Ingredients

I was a bit caught off guard during the COVID pandemic at people's mistrust of the vaccine—a solution that reopened the world and brought the pandemic under control.

There was a great deal of mistrust about what was in it. I acknowledge that I might place too much trust in our institutions such as World Health Organization, Food and Drug Administration, and American Medical Association.

But in all fairness, and perhaps with a bit of gratitude, I was awakened to the idea that we really do not know what is in anything.

I thought it might be interesting to research what is in a fly pattern. For this investigation, I chose the very well-known dry fly Adams pattern as a springboard for my materials and ingredients research. I chose this fly pattern because the Adams has been considered one of the most popular, versatile, effective, and best-selling dry fly since its creation.

The pattern requires a dry fly hook, gray thread, synthetic dubbing, hen grizzle cape feathers for wings, rooster grizzle and brown cape feathers, and head cement.

My ingredient lists below, researched though various internet rabbit holes, are as nonsensical as the evidence used by vaccine naysayers posing as experts on social media.

03. Ingredients

I was a bit caught off guard during the COVID pandemic at people's mistrust of the vaccine—a solution that reopened the world and brought the pandemic under control.

There was a great deal of mistrust about what was in it. I acknowledge that I might place too much trust in our institutions such as World Health Organization, Food and Drug Administration, and American Medical Association.

But in all fairness, and perhaps with a bit of gratitude, I was awakened to the idea that we really do not know what is in anything.

I thought it might be interesting to research what is in a fly pattern. For this investigation, I chose the very well-known dry fly Adams pattern as a springboard for my materials and ingredients research. I chose this fly pattern because the Adams has been considered one of the most popular, versatile, effective, and best-selling dry fly since its creation.

The pattern requires a dry fly hook, gray thread, synthetic dubbing, hen grizzle cape feathers for wings, rooster grizzle and brown cape feathers, and head cement.

My ingredient lists below, researched though varies internet rabbit holes, are as nonsensical as the evidence used by vaccine naysayers posing as experts on social media.

Ingredients

Hook - Dry fly TMC 100 sz 18
High-Carbon Steel
Iron (Fe)
Carbon
Hydrocarbons (CH4)
Nonfood grade mineral oil
Alkanes
Cycloalkanes
polycyclic aromatic hydrocarbons
Acetic acid
Sulfuric acid
Manganese
Vanadium

Thread flat nylon gray
Polyamides
Thermoplastic
Hexamethylene diamine
Adipic acid (diacid)
(CONH)
Coal
Air
Water
Adipic acid (diacid)
Bees wax
Paraffin

Tail and Wings Hackle
Rooster and hen grizzly cape
hackle feathers
Keratin
Peroxide
Denatured alcohol
Borax (banned in EU)
Hydrated or anhydrous borate of
sodium
Calcium
Ash
Crude Protein
Lysine crude fat
Crude Fiber
Manganese
Bacillus subtills
Bacillus licheniformis
Pyridoxine Hydrochloride
Manganous Oxide
Riboflavin
Yucca schidigera
Sodium Aluminosilicate
Menadione Sodium Bisulfite
Copper sulfate
Tagetes
Sodium Tetraborate

Aminoglycosides
Chlorotetracycline (CTC)
Oxytetracycline (OTC)
Bambermycin
Beta-lactams
Penicillin
Cephalosporins)
Ionophores Lincosamides
Tetracycline

Body
Supper fine dubbing Adams gray
60-micron polyester
Synthetic pigments
Purified terephthalic acid (PTA)
Monotheluene glycol (MEG)
Ethylene
Inorganic pigments
Coal Tars
Petrochemicals
Possibly pigments for
copper sulfate
mercury sulfide
chromium iodide
lead oxide,
and aluminum bromide.

Cement
Lacquer
Banned in California
Cotton
Nitric acid
Sulfuric acid
Nitrocellulose
Cellulose acetate butyrate
Acrylic resigns
Methyl methacrylate
monomers
Methanol I {Methyl alcohol;
Carbinol; Wood alcohol}
Toluene {Benzene, Methyl-; Toluol}
Acetone {2-Propanone}
Ethanol, 2-Butoxy- {Ethylene glycol
n-butyl
ether, (a glycol ether)}
Acetic acid, ethyl ester {Ethyl
acetate}
Light aliphatic solvent naphtha
(petroleum)

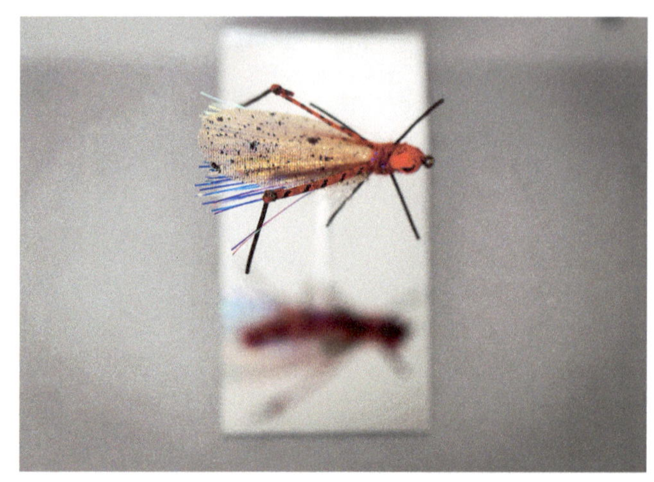

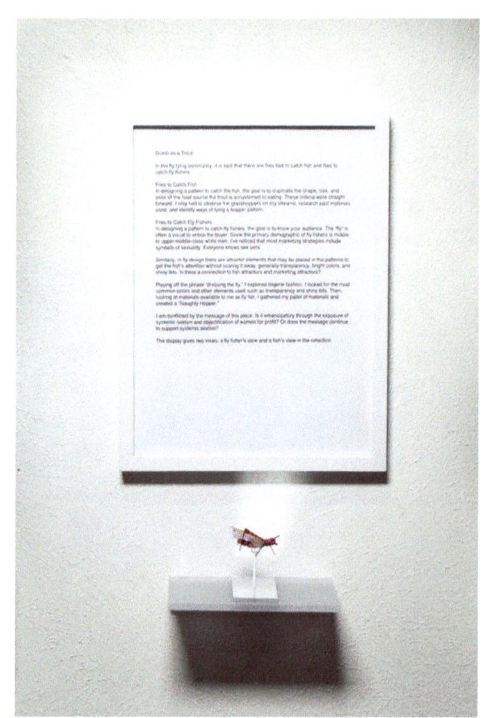

Dumb as a Trout

In the fly tying community, it is said that there are flies tied to catch fish and flies to catch fly fishers.

Flies to Catch Fish
In designing a pattern to catch the fish, the goal is to duplicate the shape, size, and color of the food source the trout is accustomed to eating. These criteria were straight forward. I only had to observe the grasshoppers on my streams, research past materials used, and identify ways of tying a hopper pattern.

Flies to Catch Fly Fishers
In designing a pattern to catch fly fishers, the goal is to know your audience. The "fly" is often a visual to entice the buyer. Since the primary demographic of fly fishers is middle to upper middle-class white men, I've noticed that most marketing strategies include symbols of sexuality. Everyone knows sex sells.

Similarly, in fly design there are attractor elements that may be placed in the patterns to get the fish's attention without scaring it away, generally transparency, bright colors, and shiny bits. Is there a connection to fish attractors and marketing attractors?

Playing off the phrase 'dressing the fly,' I explored lingerie fashion. I looked for the most common colors and other elements used such as transparency and shiny bits. Then, looking at materials available to me as fly tier, I gathered my pallet of materials and created a "Naughty Hopper."

I am conflicted by the message of this piece. Is it emancipatory through the exposure of systemic sexism and objectification of women for profit? Or does the message continue to support systemic sexism?

The display gives two views: a fly fisher's view and a fish's view in the reflection.

04. Dumb as a Trout

In the fly tying community, it is said that there are flies tied to catch fish and flies to catch fly fishers.

Flies to Catch Fish
In designing a pattern to catch the fish, the goal is to duplicate the shape, size, and color of the food source the trout is accustomed to eating. These criteria were straight forward. I only had to observe the grasshoppers on my streams, research past materials used, and identify ways of tying a hopper pattern.

Flies to Catch Fly Fishers
In designing a pattern to catch fly fishers, the goal is to know your audience. The "fly" is often a visual to entice the buyer. Since the primary demographic of fly fishers is middle- to upper-middle-class white men, I've noticed that most marketing strategies include symbols of sexuality. Everyone knows sex sells.

Similarly, in fly design there are attractor elements that may be placed in the patterns to get the fish's attention without scaring it away, generally transparency, bright colors, and shiny bits. Is there a connection to fish attractors and marketing attractors?

Playing off the phrase "dressing the fly," I explored lingerie fashion. I looked for the most common colors and other elements used such as transparency and shiny bits. Then, looking at materials available to me as fly tier, I gathered my pallet of materials and created a "Naughty Hopper."

I am conflicted by the message of this piece. Is it emancipatory through the exposure of systemic sexism and objectification of women for profit? Or does the message continue to support systemic sexism?

The display gives two views: a fly fisher's view and a fish's view in the reflection.

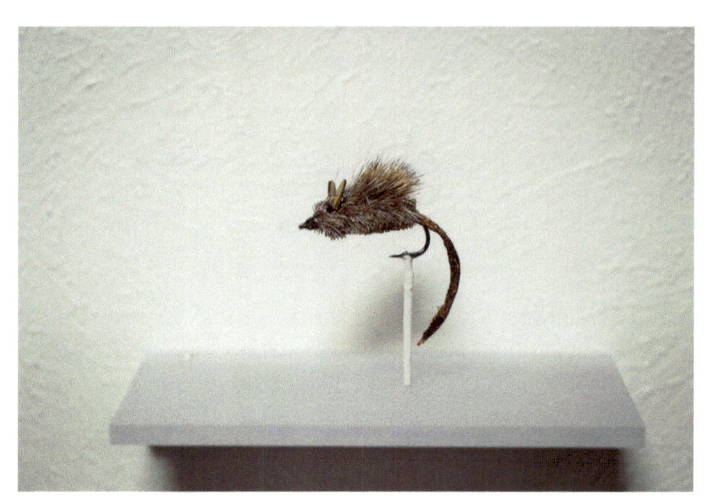

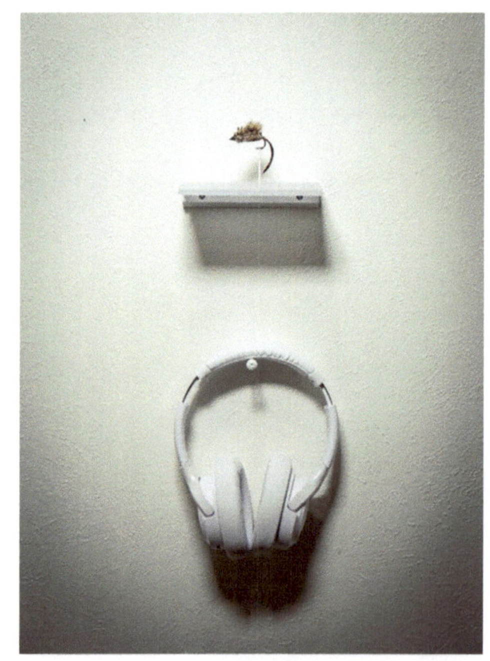

05. Evan's Mouse

Link to audio

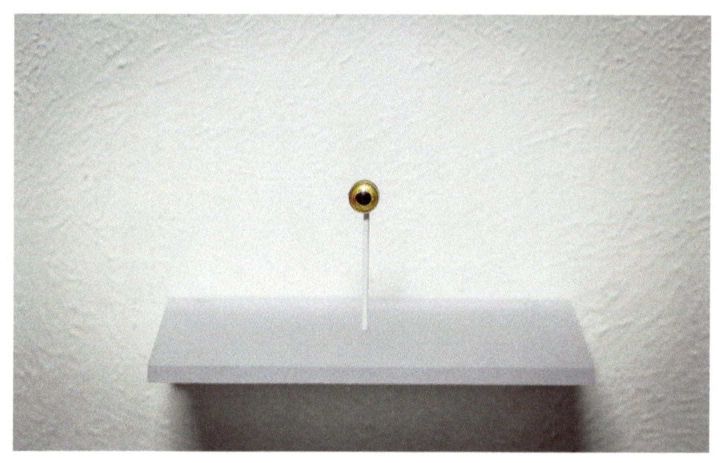

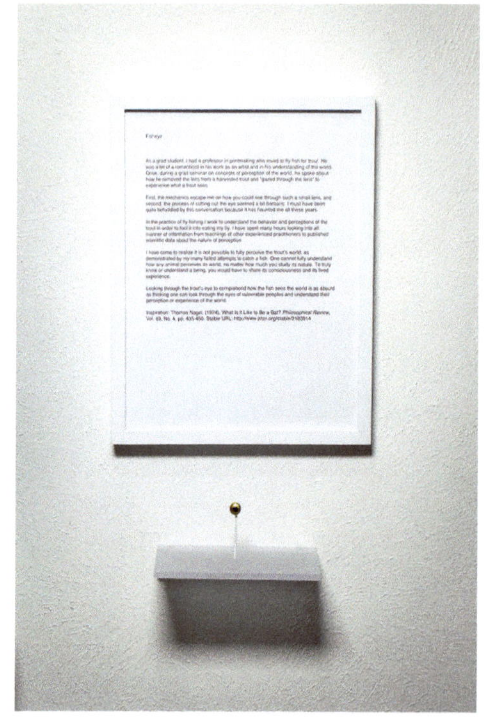

Fisheye

As a grad student, I had a professor in printmaking who loved to fly fish for trout. He was a bit of a romanticist in his work as an artist and in his understanding of the world. Once, during a grad seminar on concepts of perception of the world, he spoke about how he removed the lens from a harvested trout and "gazed through the lens" to experience what a trout sees.

First, the mechanics escape me on how you could see through such a small lens, and second, the process of cutting out the eye seemed a bit barbaric. I must have been quite befuddled by this conversation because it has haunted me all these years.

In the practice of fly fishing I work to understand the behavior and perceptions of the trout in order to fool it into eating my fly. I have spent many hours looking into all manner of information from teachings of other experienced practitioners to published scientific data about the nature of perception.

I have come to realize it is not possible to fully perceive the trout's world, as demonstrated by my many failed attempts to catch a fish. One cannot fully understand how any animal perceives its world, no matter how much you study its nature. To truly know or understand a being, you would have to share its consciousness and its lived experience.

Looking through the trout's eye to comprehend how the fish sees the world is as absurd as thinking one can look through the eyes of vulnerable peoples and understand their perception or experience of the world.

Inspiration: Thomas Nagel. (1974). What Is It Like to Be a Bat? Philosophical Review, Vol. 83, No. 4, pp. 435-450. Stable URL: http://www.jstor.org/stable/2183914

06. Fish Eye

As a grad student, I had a professor in printmaking who loved to fly fish for trout. He was a bit of a romanticist in his work as an artist and in his understanding of the world. Once, during a grad seminar on concepts of perception of the world, he spoke about how he removed the lens from a harvested trout and "gazed through the lens" to experience what a trout sees.

First, the mechanics escape me on how you could see through such a small lens, and second, the process of cutting out the eye seemed a bit barbaric. I must have been quite befuddled by this conversation because it has haunted me all these years.

In the practice of fly fishing I work to understand the behavior and perceptions of the trout in order to fool it into eating my fly. I have spent many hours looking into all manner of information from teachings of other experienced practitioners to published scientific data about the nature of perception.

I have come to realize it is not possible to fully perceive the trout's world, as demonstrated by my many failed attempts to catch a fish. One cannot fully understand how any animal perceives its world, no matter how much you study its nature. To truly know or understand a being, you would have to share its consciousness and its lived experience.

Looking through the trout's eye to comprehend how the fish sees the world is as absurd as thinking one can look through the eyes of vulnerable peoples and understand their perception or experience of the world.

Inspiration: Thomas Nagel, (1974), What Is It Like to Be a Bat? *Philosophical Review,* Vol. 83, No. 4, pp. 435-450. Stable URL: http://www.jstor.org/stable/21839

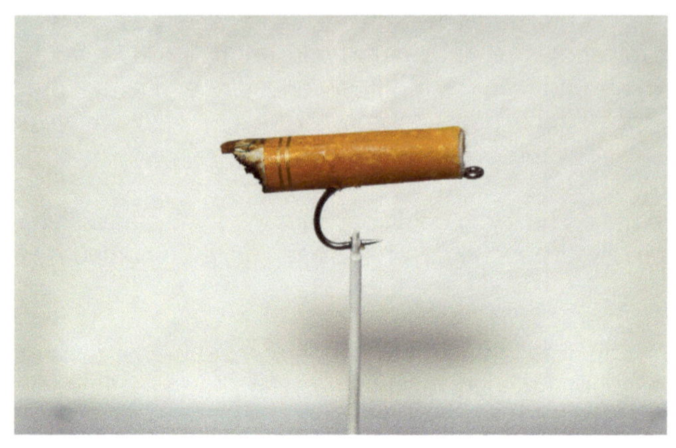

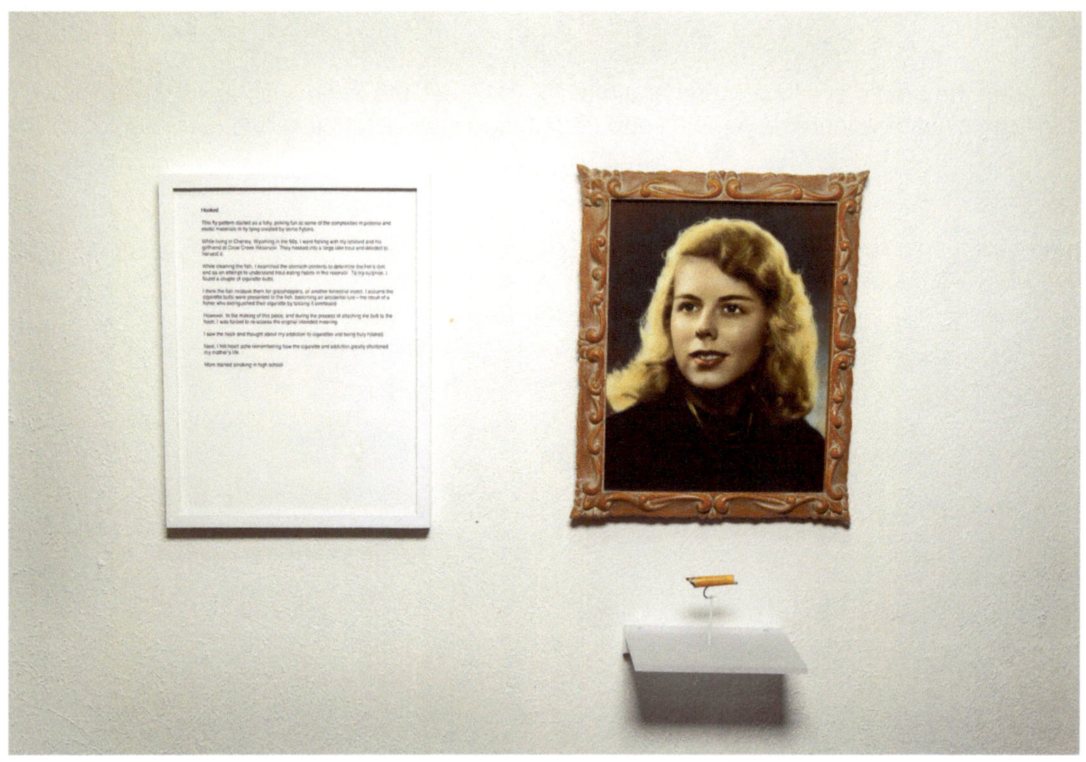
Hooked

This fly pattern started as a folly, poking fun at some of the complexities in patterns and exotic materials in fly tying created by some flytiers.

While living in Cheney, Wyoming in the 90s, I went fishing with my stepdad and his girlfriend at Crow Creek Reservoir. They hooked into a large lake trout and decided to harvest it.

While cleaning the fish, I examined the stomach contents to determine the fish's diet, and as an attempt to understand trout eating habits in this reservoir. To my surprise, I found a couple of cigarette butts.

I think the fish mistook them for grasshoppers, or another terrestrial insect. I assume the cigarette butts were presented to the fish, becoming an accidental lure – the result of a fisher who extinguished their cigarette by tossing it overboard.

However, in the making of this piece, and during the process of attaching the butt to the hook, I was forced to re-access the original intended meaning.

I saw the hook and thought about my addiction to cigarettes and being truly hooked.

Next, I felt heart ache remembering how the cigarette and addiction greatly shortened my mother's life.

Mom started smoking in high school.

07. Hooked

This fly pattern started as a folly, poking fun at some of the complexities in process and exotic materials in fly tying created by some fly-tiers.

While living in Cheney, Wyoming in the 90s, I went fishing with my landlord and his girlfriend at Crow Creek Reservoir. They hooked into a large lake trout and decided to harvest it.

While cleaning the fish, I examined the stomach contents to determine the fish's diet, and as an attempt to understand trout eating habits in this reservoir. To my surprise, I found a couple of cigarette butts.

I think the fish mistook them for grasshoppers, or another terrestrial insect. I assume the cigarette butts were presented to the fish, becoming an accidental lure—the result of a fisher who extinguished their cigarette by tossing it overboard.

However, In the making of this piece, and during the process of attaching the butt to the hook, I was forced to re-access the original intended meaning.

I saw the hook and thought about my addiction to cigarettes and being truly hooked.

Next, I felt heart ache remembering how the cigarette and addiction greatly shortened my mother's life.

Mom started smoking in high school.

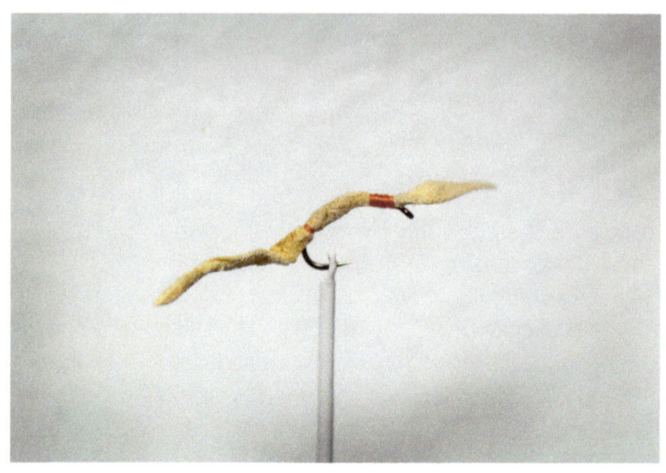

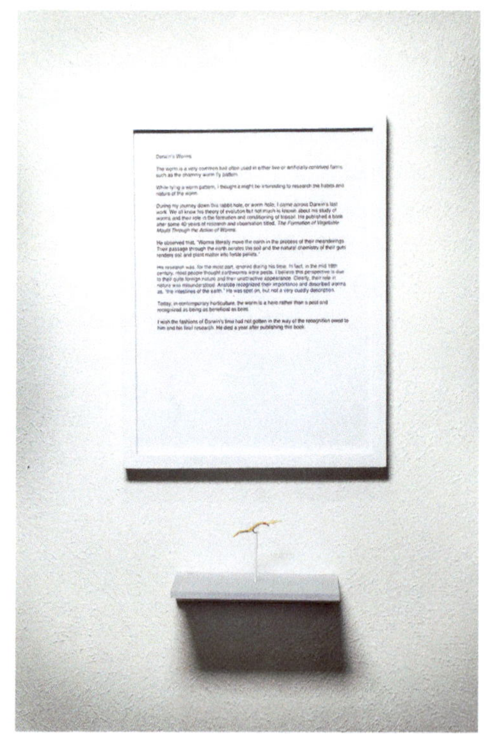

Darwin's Worms

The worm is a very common bait often used in either live or artificially contrived forms, such as the chammy worm fly pattern.

While tying a worm pattern, I thought it might be interesting to research the habits and nature of the worm.

During my journey down this rabbit hole, or worm hole, I came across Darwin's last work. We all know his theory of evolution but not much is known about his study of worms, and their role in the formation and conditioning of topsoil. He published a book after some 40 years of research and observation titled, *The Formation of Vegetable Mould Through the Action of Worms*.

He observed that, "Worms literally move the earth in the process of their meanderings. Their passage through the earth aerates the soil and the natural chemistry of their guts renders soil and plant matter into fertile pellets."

His research was, for the most part, ignored during his time. In fact, in the mid 19th century, most people thought earthworms were pests. I believe this perspective is due to their quite foreign nature and their unattractive appearance. Clearly, their role in nature was misunderstood. Aristotle recognized their importance and described worms as, "the intestines of the earth." He was spot on, but not a very cuddly description.

Today, in contemporary horticulture, the worm is a hero rather than a pest and recognized as being as beneficial as bees.

I wish the fashions of Darwin's time had not gotten in the way of the recognition owed to him and his final research. He died a year after publishing this book.

08. Darwin's Worms

The worm is a very common bait often used in either live or artificially contrived forms such as the chammy worm fly pattern.

While tying a worm pattern, I thought it might be interesting to research the habits and nature of the worm.

During my journey down this rabbit hole, or worm hole, I came across Darwin's last work. We all know his theory of evolution but not much is known about his study of worms and their role in the formation and conditioning of topsoil. He published a book after some 40 years of research and observation titled, *The Formation of Vegetable Mould Through the Action of Worms.*

He observed that, "Worms literally move the earth in the process of their meanderings. Their passage through the earth aerates the soil and the natural chemistry of their guts renders soil and plant matter into fertile pellets."

His research was, for the most part, ignored during his time. In fact, in the mid 19th century, most people thought earthworms were pests. I believe this perspective is due to their quite foreign nature and their unattractive appearance. Clearly, their role in nature was misunderstood. Aristotle recognized their importance and described worms as, "the intestines of the earth." He was spot on, but not a very cuddly description.

Today, in contemporary horticulture, the worm is a hero rather than a pest and recognized as being as beneficial as bees.

I wish the fashions of Darwin's time had not gotten in the way of the recognition owed to him and his final research. He died a year after publishing this book.

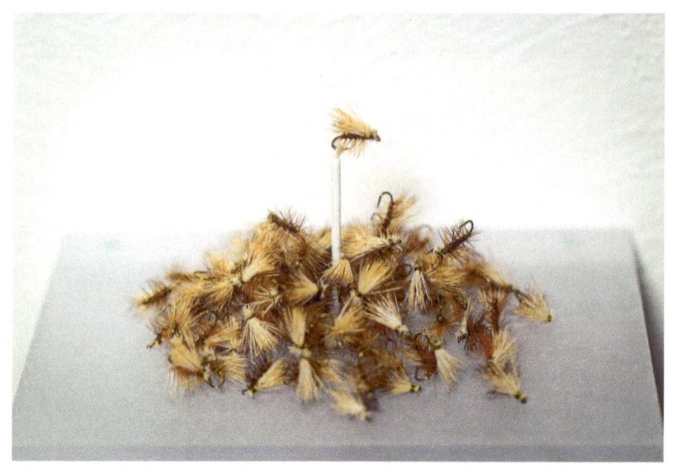

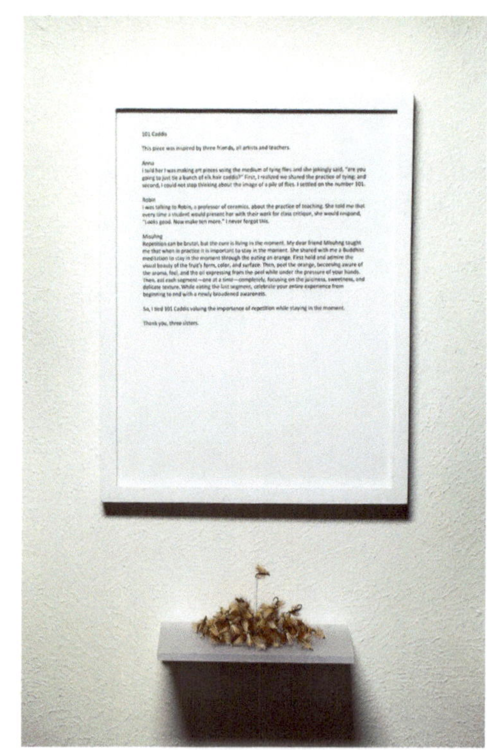

101 Caddis

This piece was inspired by three friends, all artists and teachers.

Anna
I told her I was making art pieces using the medium of tying flies and she jokingly said, "are you going to just tie a bunch of elk hair caddis?" First, I realized we shared the practice of tying; and second, I could not stop thinking about the image of a pile of flies. I settled on the number 101.

Robin
I was talking to Robin, a professor of ceramics, about the practice of teaching. She told me that every time a student would present her with their work for class critique, she would respond, "Looks good. Now make ten more." I never forgot this.

Misuhng
Repetition can be brutal, but the cure is living in the moment. My dear friend Misuhng taught me that when in practice it is important to stay in the moment. She shared with me a Buddhist meditation to stay in the moment through the eating an orange. First hold and admire the visual beauty of the fruit's form, color, and surface. Then, peel the orange, becoming aware of the aroma, feel, and the oil expressing from the peel while under the pressure of your hands. Then, eat each segment—one at a time—completely, focusing on the juiciness, sweetness, and delicate texture. While eating the last segment, celebrate your entire experience from beginning to end with a newly broadened awareness.

So, I tied 101 Caddis valuing the importance of repetition while staying in the moment.

Thank you, three sisters.

09. 101 Caddis

This piece was inspired by three friends, all artists and teachers.

Anna
I told her I was making art pieces using the medium of tying flies and she jokingly said, "are you going to just tie a bunch of elk hair caddis?" First, I realized we shared the practice of tying; and second, I could not stop thinking about the image of a pile of flies. I settled on the number 101.

Robin
I was talking to Robin, a professor of ceramics, about the practice of teaching. She told me that every time a student would present her with their work for class critique, she would respond, "Looks good. Now make ten more." I never forgot this.

Misuhng
Repetition can be brutal, but the cure is living in the moment. My dear friend Misuhng taught me that when in practice it is important to stay in the moment. She shared with me a Buddhist meditation to stay in the moment through the eating an orange. First hold and admire the visual beauty of the fruit's form, color, and surface. Then, peel the orange, becoming aware of the aroma, feel, and the oil expressing from the peel while under the pressure of your hands. Then, eat each segment—one at a time—completely, focusing on the juiciness, sweetness, and delicate texture. While eating the last segment, celebrate your entire experience from beginning to end with a newly broadened awareness.

So, I tied 101 Caddis valuing the importance of repetition while staying in the moment.

Thank you, three sisters.

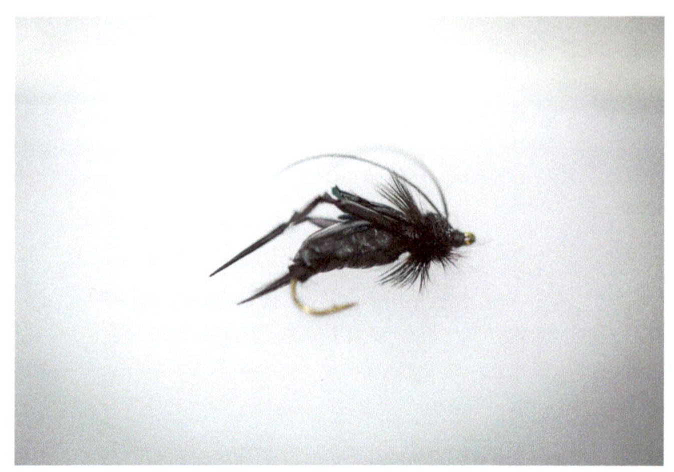

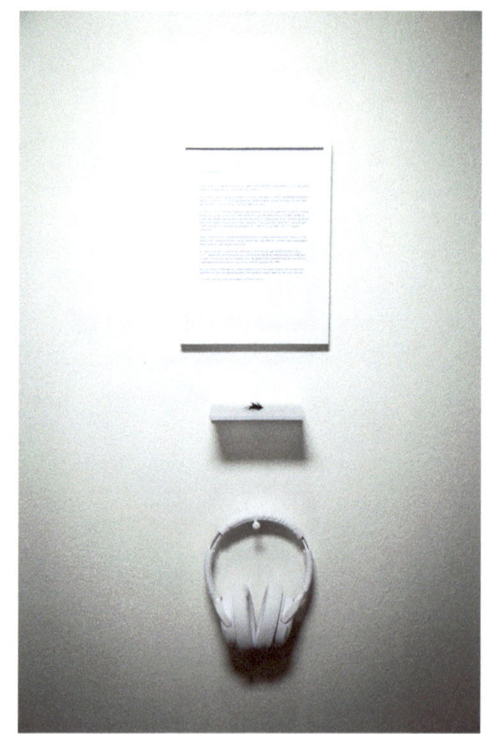

10. Cricket Swan Song

In searching for a new fly pattern to tie, I came upon a McPhail cricket pattern. So, as part of my regular practice, I researched the cricket.

The cricket is quite a marvel. It includes more than 2,400 species, with a worldwide distribution. Therefore, almost everyone on planet has experienced its musical chirping, primarily from the males attempting to attract mates and define territory.

The cricket is a shy creature, its presence almost always detected auditorily through its chirping. When I was young, I heard many a folktale from my grandparents about a cricket's ability to predict the weather and reveal the outside temperature. I discovered, in my research, an actual formula for how to interpret the cricket's message. If you count the chirps for 15 seconds and add 40, you get the Fahrenheit temperature. So, 1 chirp in 15 seconds + 40 = 55 degrees Fahrenheit.

When I think about the natural world and temperature, global warming and its impacts on the natural order inevitably surface. Having children has intensified my concerns and I worry about global warming's apocalyptic implications.

So, I went dark and researched the temperature that kills our species and found it is about 122°F. I applied the above formula. For a cricket to broadcast this temperature, it would have to chirp 5.4 chirps per second. However, this calculation is only hypothetical since the cricket's swansong would come sooner than ours as most die between 96-100°F.

Art is not science, although the creative process is much the same. Science seems a bit more restrictive to me in messaging because it must abide by natural laws. Art has more latitude.

Link to audio

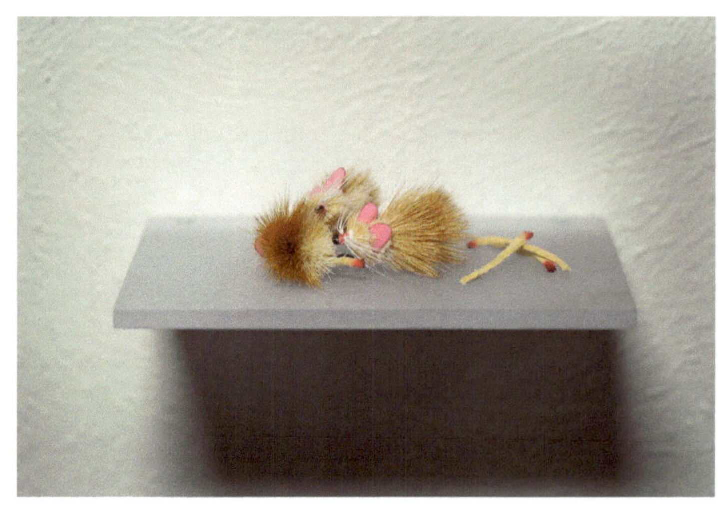

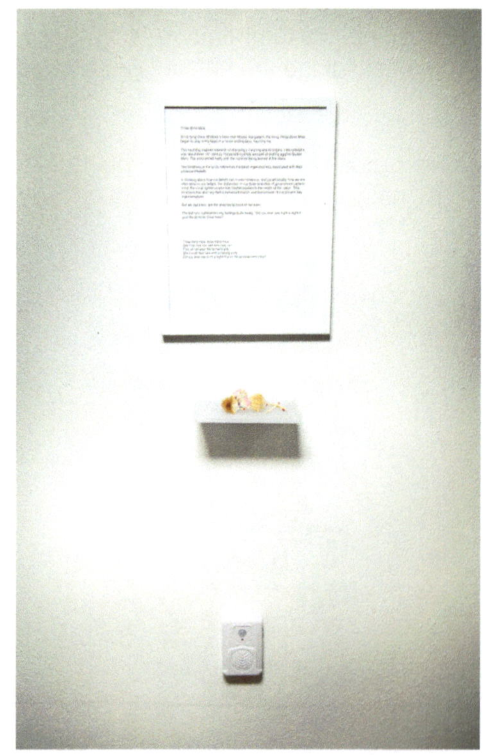

11. Three Blind Mice

While tying Dave Whitlock's Deer Hair Mouse Rat pattern, the song Three Blind Mice began to play in my head in a never-ending loop, haunting me.

This haunting inspired research on the song's meaning and its origins. I discovered it was about three 16th century Protestant loyalists accused of plotting against Queen Mary. The story ended badly with the loyalists being burned at the stake.

The blindness in the lyrics references the blind impetuousness associated with their protestant beliefs.

In thinking about how our beliefs can create blindness, and paradoxically, how we are often blind to our beliefs, the disfunction in our three branches of government came to mind. Personal righteousness has blinded leaders to the needs of the nation. This blindness has also resulted in extrema tribalism and divisiveness of our present-day representatives.

But we, not them, are the ones being burnt at the stake.

The last lyric summarizes my feelings quite nicely, "Did you ever see such a sight in your life as three blind mice?"

Three blind mice, three blind mice
See how they run, see how they run
They all ran after the farmer's wife
She cut off their tails with a carving knife
Did you ever see such a sight in your life as three blind mice?

Link to audio

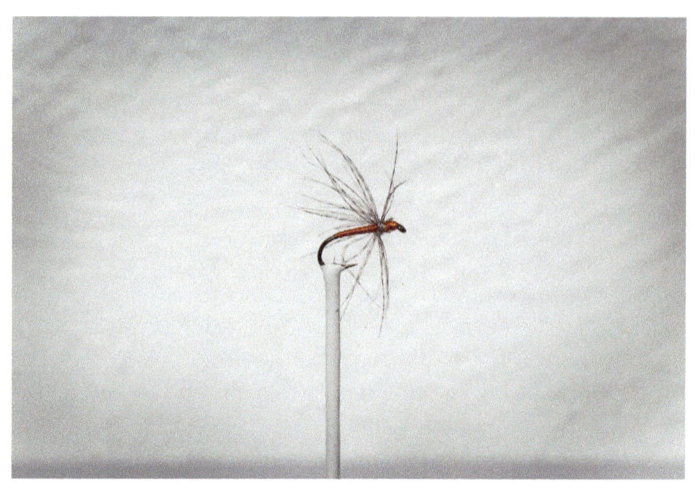

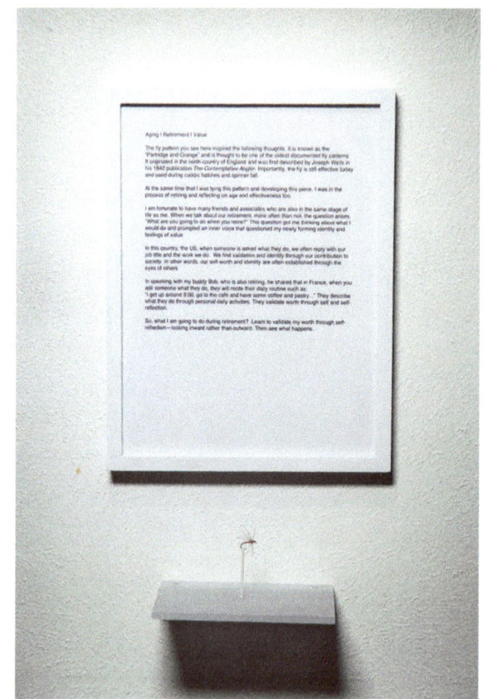

Aging | Retirement | Value

The fly pattern you see here inspired the following thoughts. It is known as the "Partridge and Orange" and is thought to be one of the oldest documented fly patterns. It originated in the north country of England and was first described by Joseph Wells in his 1842 publication The Contemplative Angler. Importantly, the fly is still effective today and used during caddis hatches and spinner fall.

At the same time that I was tying this pattern and developing this piece, I was in the process of retiring and reflecting on age and effectiveness too.

I am fortunate to have many friends and associates who are also in the same stage of life as me. When we talk about our retirement, more often than not, the question arises, "What are you going to do when you retire?" This question got me thinking about what I would do and prompted an inner voice that questioned my newly forming identity and feelings of value.

In this country, the US, when someone is asked what they do, we often reply with our job title and the work we do. We find validation and identity through our contribution to society. In other words, our self-worth and identity are often established through the eyes of others.

In speaking with my buddy Bob, who is also retiring, he shared that in France, when you ask someone what they do, they will recite their daily routine such as:
"I get up around 9:00, go to the cafe and have some coffee and pastry..." They describe what they do through personal daily activities. They validate worth through self and self-reflection.

So, what I am going to do during retirement? Learn to validate my worth through self-reflection—looking inward rather than outward. Then see what happens.

12. Aging | Retirement | Value

The fly pattern you see here inspired the following thoughts. It is known as the "Partridge and Orange" and is thought to be one of the oldest documented fly patterns. It originated in the north country of England and was first described by Joseph Wells in his 1842 publication The Contemplative Angler. Importantly, the fly is still effective today and used during caddis hatches and spinner fall.

At the same time that I was tying this pattern and developing this piece, I was in the process of retiring and reflecting on age and effectiveness too.

I am fortunate to have many friends and associates who are also in the same stage of life as me. When we talk about our retirement, more often than not, the question arises, "What are you going to do when you retire?" This question got me thinking about what I would do and prompted an inner voice that questioned my newly forming identity and feelings of value.

In this country, the US, when someone is asked what they do, we often reply with our job title and the work we do. We find validation and identity through our contribution to society. In other words, our self-worth and identity are often established through the eyes of others.

In speaking with my buddy Bob, who is also retiring, he shared that in France, when you ask someone what they do, they will recite their daily routine such as: "I get up around 9:00, go to the café and have some coffee and pastry..." They describe what they do through personal daily activities. They validate worth through self and self-reflection.

So, what I am going to do during retirement? Learn to validate my worth through self-reflection—looking inward rather than outward. Then see what happens.

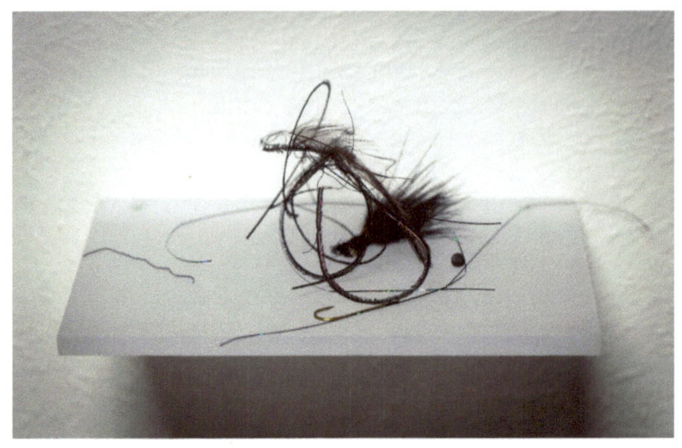

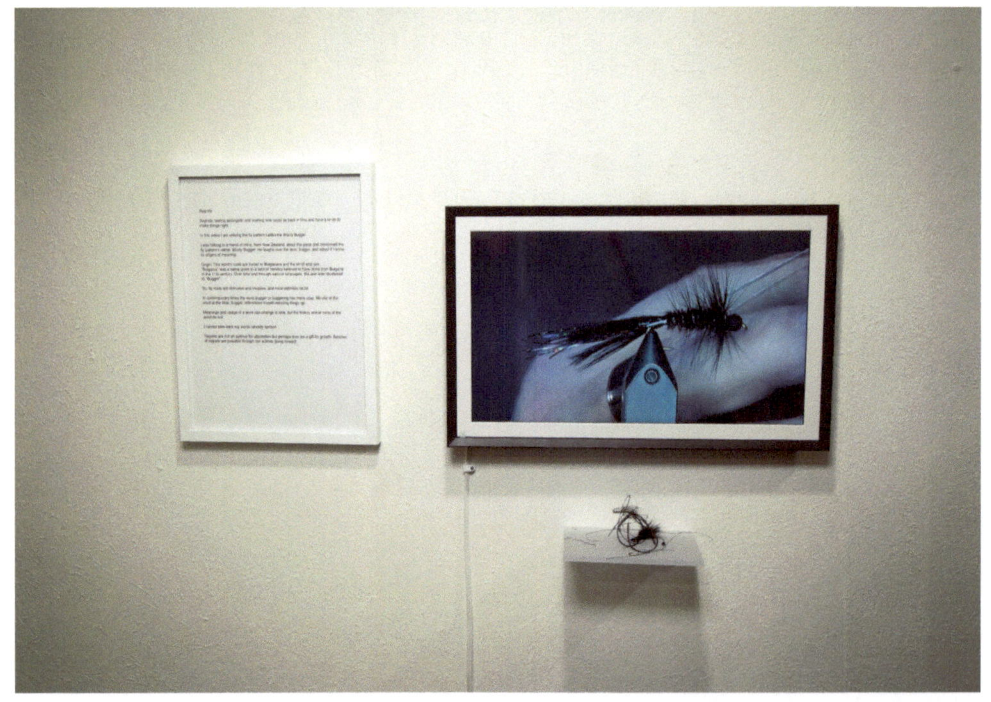

13. Regret

Regret: Feeling apologetic and wishing one could go back in time and have a re-do to make things right.

In this video I am untying the fly pattern called the Wooly Bugger.

I was talking to a friend of mine, from New Zealand, about this piece and mentioned the fly pattern's name, Wooly Bugger. He laughed over the term bugger and asked if I knew the origins of its meaning.

Origin: The roots of bugger are traced back to the Bulgarians. "Bulgarus" was a name given to a sect of abusive heretics believed to have come from Bulgaria in the 11th century. Over time and through various languages, it was later shortened to the slur "bugger." So, its roots are obtrusive and invasive, and most certainly racist.

In contemporary times the word bugger or buggering has many uses. It currently has many meanings ranging from the description of an abusive man to feeling sympathy for another who has experienced bad luck. My use of bugger at the time was offensive to my New Zealand colleague and regret having used it.

Meanings and word usage can change over time, but the history and roots of the word do not.

I cannot take back my words already spoken. Regrets are not an avenue for absolution but perhaps they are a gift for growth.

Link to video
(no audio)

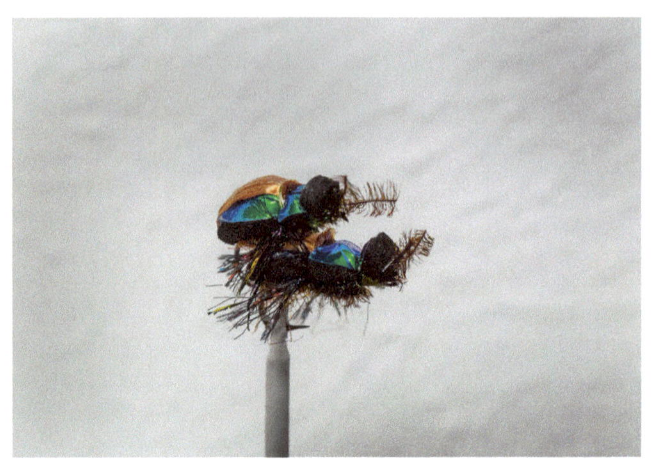

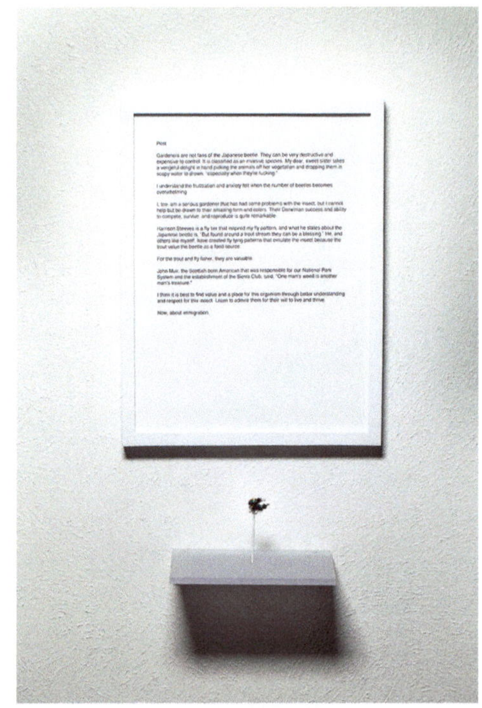

Pest

Gardeners are not fans of the *Japanese beetle*. They can be very destructive and expensive to control. It is classified as an invasive species. My dear, sweet sister takes a vengeful delight in hand pulling the animals off her vegetation and dropping them in soapy water to drown, "especially when they're fucking."

I understand the frustration and anxiety felt when the number of beetles becomes overwhelming.

I, too, am a serious gardener that has had some problems with the insect, but I cannot help but be drawn to their amazing form and colors. Their Darwinian success and ability to compete, survive, and reproduce is quite remarkable.

Harrison Steeves is a fly tier that inspired my fly pattern, and what he states about the Japanese beetle is, "But found around a trout stream they can be a blessing." He, and others like myself, have created fly tying patterns that emulate the insect because the trout value the beetle as a food source.

For the trout and fly fisher, they are valuable.

John Muir, the Scottish born American that was responsible for our National Park System and the establishment of the Sierra Club, said, "One man's weed is another man's treasure."

I think it is best to find value and a place for this organism through better understanding and respect for this insect. Learn to admire them for their will to live and thrive.

Now, about emmigration.

14. Pest

Gardeners are not fans of the Japanese beetle. They can be very destructive and expensive to control. It is classified as an invasive species. My dear, sweet sister takes a vengeful delight in hand picking the animals off her vegetation and dropping them in soapy water to drown, "especially when they're fucking."

I understand the frustration and anxiety felt when the number of beetles becomes overwhelming.

I, too, am a serious gardener that has had some problems with the insect, but I cannot help but be drawn to their amazing form and colors. Their Darwinian success and ability to compete, survive, and reproduce is quite remarkable.

Harrison Steeves is a fly tier that inspired my fly pattern, and what he states about the Japanese beetle is, "But found around a trout stream they can be a blessing." He, and others like myself, have created fly tying patterns that emulate the insect because the trout value the beetle as a food source.

For the trout and fly fisher, they are valuable.

John Muir, the Scottish born American that was responsible for our National Park System and the establishment of the Sierra Club, said, "One man's weed is another man's treasure."

I think it is best to find value and a place for this organism through better understanding and respect for this insect. Learn to admire them for their will to live and thrive.

Now, about immigration.

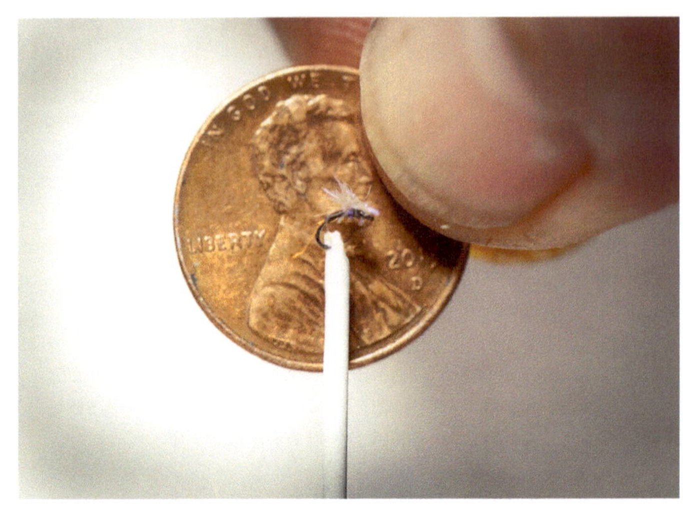

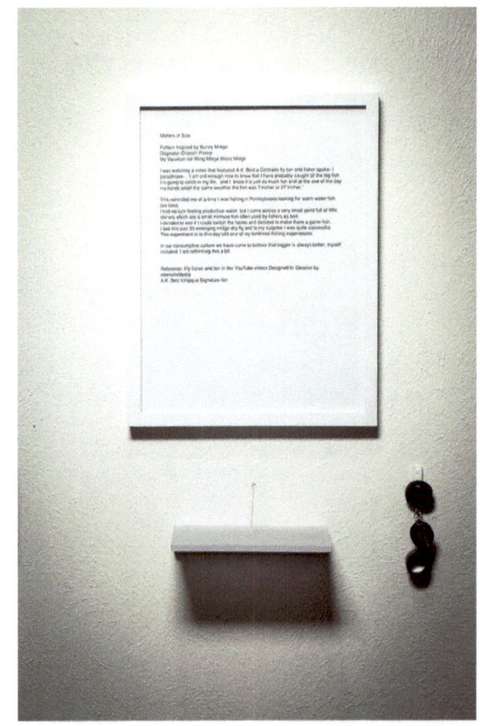

Matters of Size

Pattern Inspired by Bunny Midge
Originator-Cheech Pierce
My Variation on Wing Midge Mono Midge

I was watching a video that featured A.K. Best a Colorado fly tier and fisher spoke- I paraphrase- , I am old enough now to know that I have probably caught all the big fish I'm going to catch in my life, and I know it is just as much fun and at the end of the day my hands smell the same weather the fish was 7 inches or 27 inches."

This reminded me of a time I was fishing in Pennsylvania looking for warm water fish like bass.
I had no luck finding productive water, but I came across a very small pond full of little shiners which are a small minnow fish often used by fishers as bait.
I decided to see if I could switch the tables and decided to make them a game fish.
I tied this size 30 emerging midge dry fly and to my surprise I was quite successful.
This experiment is to this day still one of my fondness fishing experiences.

In our consumptive culture we have come to believe that bigger is always better, myself included. I am rethinking this a bit.

Reference: Fly fisher and tier in the YouTube videos Designed in Deceiver by etensolidMedia
A.K. Best Umpqua Signature tier

15. Matters of Size

Anyone that has been involved in the fishing experience has been exposed to bragging; sharing stories about the biggest fish ever caught, usually exaggerated.

I watched a video featuring a Colorado fly tier and fisher, A.K. Best. He spoke about the importance of catching a big fish. He says, "I am old enough now to know that I have probably caught all the big fish I'm going to catch in my life. I now know it is just as much fun, and at the end of the day my hands smell the same, whether the fish was a 7 incher or a 27 incher."

This story reminded me of a time when I was fishing for bass in Pennsylvania. I had no luck finding productive water, but during my quest I came across a very small pond full of little shiners, which are a small minnow fish often used by fishers as bait.

I decided to see if I could turn the tables and rather than thinking of the shiners as bait, I decided to pursue them as game fish. I tied this size 30 emerging midge dry fly, and to my surprise, the fly was quite successful. To this day, this fishing experience is one of my fondest fishing memories.

Bigger is not always better.

Author Biography

William Jude Rumley (b. 1957, Minneapolis, Minnesota) moved at age of three to Denver, Colorado.

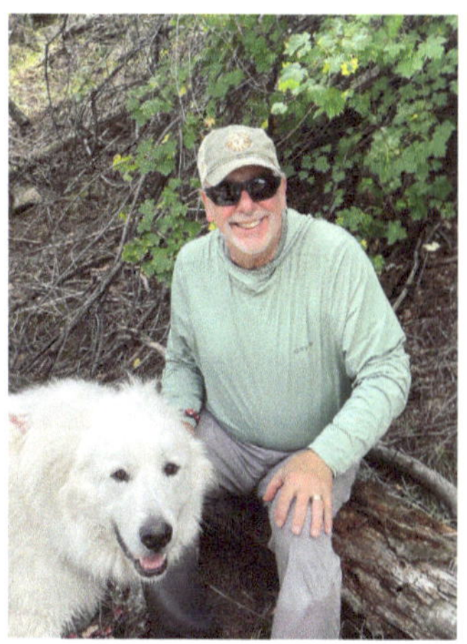

Began at Arapahoe Community College studying biology, then transferred to the University of Denver to earn his Bachelor of Fine Arts degree in photography in 1981. While working as a public relations photographer and a full-time professional chef, he suffered a career-interrupting injury while cooking. He then applied and was accepted into the MFA program at the University of Denver. He began using all his past experiences, including working as a chef, performing in theater, and mastering photography and other indexical media. Explored multimedia methods of communication through installation and performance, thematically focused on social constructs. He earned his Master of Fine Arts in 1985 from the University of Denver.

Rumley has exhibited his works and installations nationally in many venues, including the Alternative Art Museum and Amos Eno Gallery in New York City. He was a member and exhibiter at Nexus Foundation for Todays Art and exhibited at the Philadelphia Art Alliance, and Moore College of Art. In the Denver area he has exhibited at the Denver Art Museum, Civic Center, University of Colorado-Boulder, Pirate Art Oasis, Galapago Space and the Arvada Center.

Another facet to his work in the arts was his work as an exhibition preparator in Philadelphia at The Institute of Contemporary Art, Fabric Workshop, The Balch Institute for Ethnic Studies, and the Jewish Museum of American History. And in the Denver area for the Denver Art Museum, and University of Colorado Art Museum. As a preparator, he worked as an artist assistant and fabricated works for for many artist including Chuck Fallen, David Ireland, Ann Hamilton, Louise Bourgeois, and James Turrell.

In addition to his studio practice, Rumley has taught courses in the arts for University of Denver, Denver Art Museum, and Trenton State College. For the last 24 years he has worked for the University of Colorado-Boulder in the Department of Art and Art History as Director of the Woodshop as well as teaching a course in woodworking and museum practices. For more information visit rumleyart.com.

Other practices include horticulture, culinary arts, livestock care, and fly fishing.

Credits

1. Missed Opportunity, 2023, Pattern – Emerging Midge 1, Originator: Ken Iwamasa

2. Pronouns, 2023, Pattern – RuPaul Feathers 2023, Original Pattern: CJ's Mini Johnson, Originator: Chad Johnson, Variant Design: William Jude Rumley

3. Ingredients, 2024, Pattern – Adams, Original Pattern: Adams, Originator: Leonard Hallada

4. Dumb as a Trout, 2023, Pattern – Naughty Hopper, Originator: William Jude Rumley

5. Evans Mouse, 2024, Pattern – Mouse, Original Pattern: Rat / Mouse, Originator: Dave Whitlock, Variant Design: William Jude Rumley

6. Fish Eye, 2024, Glass Taxidermy Trout Eye, Design: William Jude Rumley

7. Hooked, 2023, Pattern – Bill's Butt, Originator: William Jude Rumley

8. Darwin's Worms, 2024, Pattern – Chamois Worm, Original Pattern: Chamois Worm, Originator: Guido Vinck, Variant Design: William Jude Rumley

9. 101 Caddis, 2024, Pattern – Elk Hair Caddis, Original Pattern: Elk Hair Caddis, Originator: Al Troth

10. Cricket Swan Song, 2024, Pattern – Cricket, Original Pattern: Black Cricket, Inspiration: David McPhail, Variant Design: William Jude Rumley

11. Three Blind Mice, 2024, Pattern – Blind Mouse, Original Pattern: Rat / Mouse Originator: Dave Whitlock, Variant Design: William Jude Rumley

12. Aging | Retirement | Value, 2024, Pattern – Orange and Partridge, Original Pattern: Orange and Partridge, Originator: Thomas E. Pritt, 1895

13. Regret, 2024, Original Pattern: Wooly Bugger, Originator: Russell Blessing, Variant Design: William Jude Rumley

14. Pest, 2024, Pattern – Fucking Japanese Beetle, Original Pattern: Japanese Beetle, Inspiration: Harrison Steeves, Variant Design: William Jude Rumley

15. Matters of Size, 2024, Pattern – Bunny Midge, Originator Pattern Bunny Midge, Originator: Cheech Pierce, Variant Design: William Jude Rumley

www.ingramcontent.com/pod-product-compliance
Lightning Source LLC
Chambersburg PA
CBHW040050240726
48664CB00004B/1128